Ilya Muromets
&
The Russian Knight

The Dawn of Long Range Aviation

Hugh Harkins

Copyright © 2021 Hugh Harkins FRAS, MIstP, MRAeS

All rights reserved.

ISBN: 1-903630-93-2
ISBN-13: 978-1-903630-93-8

Ilya Muromets
&
The Russian Knight

© 2021 Hugh Harkins FRAS, MIstP, MRAeS

Centurion Publishing

United Kingdom

ISBN 10: 1-903630-93-2
ISBN 13: 978-1-903630-93-8

This volume first published in 2021

The author is identified as the copyright holder of this work under sections 77 and 78 of the Copyright Designs and Patents Act 1988

Cover design © Centurion Publishing & KDP

Page layout, concept and design © Centurion Publishing

All rights reserved. No part of this publication may be reproduced, stored in a retrieval system, transmitted in any form, or by any means, electronic, mechanical or photocopied, recorded or otherwise, without the written permission of the publisher

This volume has adopted a quasi-Harvard Manual of Style for referencing. It has, however, not always been pertinent or possible to adopt a standard referencing format

CONTENTS

	Introduction	vii
1	The Grand Baltic and the Russian Knight	1
2	Ilya Muromets	13
3	Glossary	43
4	Bibliography	44

INTRODUCTION

The intent of this volume is to detail the world's premier large-size multi-engine heavier than air craft, the Grand Baltic/Russian Knight and the Ilya Muromets, the world's premier four engine heavy bomber/reconnaissance aircraft. The latter entered operations with the air service of the Imperial Russian Army in 1915 and served through the years of World War 1 – 1914 to 1918 – and the Russian Civil War that followed, from which the Soviet Union was born.

Drawing upon historical data from a number of sources, including the Ministry of Defence of the Russian Federation and the Russian Air Force (Aerospace Forces) historical records, the volume covers the genesis, design and development of the Grand Baltic, it's evolution into the Russian Knight and the subsequent development and deployment of the Ilya Muromets as a heavy bomber/reconnaissance aircraft operating against the Central Powers from 1915. It further covers the Ilya Muromets fleet organisation in the Russian Civil War and the establishment of air transport links in the early Soviet period, 1921-1922.

1

THE GRAND BALTIC AND THE RUSSIAN KNIGHT

A cursory flashback to heavy bomber operations of World War 1 throws a spotlight on several well-known names, such as the British Handley Page 0/400 (twin-engine biplane) – delivered from 1918 – the German Gotha (twin-engine biplane) – commenced operations in summer 1917 – and the Italian CA-42 (multi-engine triplane) – flown in 1916. Lost in translation of that terrible conflict and the Russian/Soviet civil war that raged for several years after the Armistice of November 1918, is the fact that the Ilya Muromets, the first large-size long-range multi-engine heavy bomber aircraft to enter service, did so in 1914 Imperial Russia.

Although Imperial Russia's Long Range Aviation, the world's premier long-range heavier than air bomber organisation, was not formally formed until 23 December 1914 (not under the Long Range Aviation label), the pioneering work conducted in the earliest days of aviation in Imperial Russia were instrumental in sowing the seeds that eventually spawned that service. Design of powered flying machines had progressed in Imperial Russia in the latter part of the nineteenth century. However, bureaucracy proved to be as problematic as technical issues. D. Voinov failed to get the Imperial Russian Minister of War to consider his design for a powered flying machine, put forward on 3 February 1887. In the event, the first powered aircraft flight in Imperial Russia took place on 19 June 1910 (6 June, old style – the Julian calendar was commonly used in Imperial Russia) when the Hackel-3 biplane (designer, J.M. Gakkel) lifted into the air (pilot, V.F. Bulgakov) at Gatchina field. A twin-engine aircraft of aluminium construction, designed by B.G. Lutsk, was flown in Russia on 24 February 1912 – this was the largest aircraft of aluminium construction that had been built at that time. Lutsk, having worked on the design of German heavier than air flying machines, had designed the Loutsky-1 (considered to be the first twin-engine aircraft design to actually attain flight status) and Loutsky-2 and Loutsky-3 aircraft (MODRF & Russian Air Force (Aerospace Forces) Historical records).

The Ilya Muromets (top) was the World's first multi-engine heavy bomber aircraft to enter serial production. This large four engine biplane was a world apart from the first patented Russian fixed wing flying machine (bottom) designed by aeronautics researcher A.F. Mozhaisky. This aircraft design, which dated back to 15 November 1881, had no official backing and failed to progress to flight status. Imperial Russia would subsequently fall behind other nations in fixed wing aeronautical development, the first such powered flight not taking place until June 1910.

The S-21 in the original Grand Baltic configuration is prepared for flight. When this aircraft debuted in 1913 it was the largest non-lighter than air technology aircraft in existence.

In the first decade of the twentieth century, airships appeared to hold more potential for development of a viable long-range air transport capability than did fixed wing aircraft. Airships also offered the means to develop a bombing capability for airborne attacks on enemy rear areas and offered potential for previously unprecedented long-range reconnaissance. Requirement for such capabilities in Imperial Russia was pushed through in a commission chaired by N.L. Kiricheva, which included a number of scientists – N.E. Zhukovsky, A.N. Krylov, V.V. Kuznetsov & E.S. Fedorov – which authorised construction of the large Merlin airship design on 22 February 1907. Development of the Merlin, Russia's first airship constructed for military purposes, was to be overseen by N.I. Utesheva. The airship, designed with a volume of 6000 m^3, was constructed of domestic material, except for the two 100 hp. motors, which were foreign sourced – a situation which would be carried over to large fixed with aircraft development. The Merlin was to pave the way for introduction of large powered heavier than air machines into specialist bomber units with the Imperial Russian Army less than a decade later (MODRF & Russian Air Force (Aerospace Forces) Historical records).

Prior to design and construction of the S-22 Ilya Muromets, experience of design and construction of large multi-engine aircraft was gained through studies for such an aircraft by Igor Sikorsky in St. Petersburg. Sikorsky, whom was born in 1889 (son of medical Professor) had studied at the St Petersburg Maritime College, then the Paris School of Engineering (1906) before being admitted to the Kiev Polytechnic Institute in 1907 until 1911. During a stay in France, Sikorsky had acquainted himself with French aircraft designs (SA10, 1913). It was whilst at the Polytechnic Institute that Sikorsky completed his early design studies for two rotary wing H-1 (1909) and H-2 (1910) and several small fixed wing aircraft. The rotary wing designs and the first of the fixed wing designs, the S-1 biplane single engine pusher of 1910, failed to attain flight – all of Sikorsky's subsequent fixed wing designs were tractor powered. There followed a series of designs that whilst they attained flight, could not be classed as anything approaching practical flight durations. The S-2 and S-3 of 1910 got airborne for only 12 seconds and 7 minutes respectively. The S-4 of 1911 was destined not to fly. The S-5 of 1911 would be Sikorsky's first aircraft that could be considered a success in regard to the practicability of its flight capabilities – the maiden flight was conducted on 17 May 1911. This design would go on to establish four aviation records within Imperial Russia. In November of the same year, an evolved design, the S-6 flew (this design could carry three persons, including the pilot). The S-7 (a two place single-engine monoplane) and S-8 (a biplane intended for training purposes) flew in 1912. The S-9 monoplane, built in 1913, did not fly. The S-10 (biplane) and S-11 and S-12 (monoplanes) flew in 1913, as did the S-15, which was a single engine biplane designed for the bombing role.

Sikorsky beside the S-21 Grand Baltic at the test field in March 1913. Although Sikorsky had designed several flying machines prior to the S-21, it was this large machine that pushed him to the fore of renowned aeronautic designers.

At the time of the S-15 design and build, Sikorsky was busy designing a far grander aircraft that could form the basis for military functions as a long-range bomber/reconnaissance aircraft or a civilian function as a passenger transport aircraft. This would emerge as the S-21 Grand Baltic (Le Grande) – which would be further developed as the first successful application of a four engine fixed-wing aircraft in the history of aviation. The S-21 was designed after Sikorsky was placed in the position of chief designer at the Baltic Carriage Works aviation department (headed by M.V. Syzdlowski) in 1912 – Sikorsky remained in this position until 1917.

Sikorsky's interest in multi-engine aircraft is said to have stemmed from his encountering engine trouble in a single engine aircraft, exciting the mantra that two or more engines would give a degree of safety against engine failure. It is most likely that there is more to it than that as the multi-engine designs that would emerge from the Baltic Carriage Works were considerably larger than the prior small single-engine designs, suggesting that increased carrying capacity and increased range were at the fore in the planning for a future serial produced multi-engine aircraft design.

The Grand Baltic, commonly referred to as the Russian Knight (Russkii Vityaz) once it was modified to have all four engines arrayed in line abreast, was of all-wood construction in regard to airframe, albeit apparently with some steel tubing enveloped by the wood and fabric coverings for the supporting surfaces and the rear fuselage section (SA10, 1913). The design, which was constructed with thought to a degree of disassembly to facilitate storage and or surface transport, featured a large differential span biplane main wing section. Wing span was put at 28 m (upper wing) with the lower wing spanning some 5.5 m less than the upper wing. Wing area was in the order of 120 m^2, the wings featuring ailerons to provide the function of lateral stability (Aeronautics, 1913). At the third set of vertical spars, vertical surfaces were positioned below the upper main wing surface, effectively ventral to the upper main wing. Each of these surfaces covered an area in the region of 1.6 m^2 (SA, 1913).

The cockpit section was furnished with two separate wheels for the pilot(s). Aft of the cockpit section was the passenger cabin/cargo section with an observation balcony forward of the cockpit. The passenger cabin, cockpit and forward observation balcony made up the forward fuselage section, which was linked to the tail section through a relatively narrow elongated boom section. Airframe length was put at 20 m from the tail to the forward observation balcony ahead of the cockpit, which was in the order of 3.05 m (~10 ft.) in length. The tail unit consisted of a single (non-biplane) horizontal surface, incorporating the tail-plane elevator. Twin vertical tail surfaces, incorporating twin-rudders, were positioned either side of the central horizontal tail section (Aeronautics, 1913 & SA, 1913). The vertical rudders, horizontal elevators and flaps/ailerons were controlled through a centrally mounted strut and wire complex.

The undercarriage consisted of a combination skid/wheel complex. The four skids, for landing, consisted of two long units beneath the fuselage with two shorter units, one each side, beneath the lower wing section. The wheel complex, for take-off and ground movement, consisted of an eight wheel chassis featuring an elastic suspension system. The respective paired wheels would be attached to the short length skids. Rubber strapping, incorporated into the bracket system, provisioned said elastic suspension, which expanded in a lateral direction (Aeronautics, 1913 & SA, 1913).

The Grand Baltic was equipped with a duel wheel/skid undercarriage complex positioned roughly central, below the enclosed cockpit/passenger cabin section.

The sturdy design of the wheels, which were disposed in pairs between the skids, combined with the power of the engines, enabled the Grand Baltic (Russian Knight), which had a normal weight of around 2700 kg, to lift a passenger/cargo load of at least 726 kg (~1,600 lb.) into the air. Other values for load carrying capability are in the order of 737 kg – this could be four passengers, which, along with up to three crew (two pilots under normal requirements), brought capacity to seven persons. Maximum take-off weight, with a full fuel and passenger/cargo load, was in the region of 3200 kg (Aeronautics, 1913 & SA 10, 1913).

The cabin(s) were enclosed to facilitate protection from the elements. The large window areas were of celluloid material (SA, 1913). Although the aircraft structure was built predominantly of wood, steel was used in certain areas, such as sheets laid on the floor of the passenger cabin and the aircraft forward section. Passengers and crew were accommodated on seats arranged in three rows, with a passageway between the two rearward rows. The two forward seats were occupied by the crew (pilots) with a control wheel and lever arrangement on the structure in front with a further control lever activated by foot movements – the wheel operated the ailerons, the forward control lever operated the rudder for elevation and the foot lever operated the vertical rudder surfaces (SA10, 1913).

At some point a wireless/telegraph transmit/receiver set was apparently installed toward the rear of the cabin. The antenna for this complex extended outward on the supporting surfaces and then rearward, ending at the tail section. The Grand Baltic (Russian Knight) could be fitted with two acetylene searchlights (SA10, 1913), one such unit appearing to be installed on the extreme fore of the observation balcony.

The S-21 in Grand Baltic and Russian Knight configurations was powered by German designed and built Argus aero engines similar to the Argus III illustrated. The Russian Knight would incorporate four such engines carried on the wings – two on each side of the fuselage. UK Air Ministry

The Grand Baltic (Russian Knight) would be powered by Argus motors (four in the Russian Knight), each developing some 100 hp. to drive two bladed wooden propellers spanning ~2.6 m (~8.6 ft.). In the original configuration the motors were apparently mounted on the lower main wing, arranged one to the fore and one aft on each of the pairs, which would give a distinct impression of a twin engine design. Conflicting evidence indicates that the aircraft was initially powered by just two engines, photographs surviving in the archives appearing to support this hypothesis. However, what is clear is that a redesign altered the power plant layout to four engines arranged to the fore of the wing as noted above, configured in two pairs of two on each side of the central flight cabin. The reconfigured engine layout was considered to be more efficient in flight and resulted in a modest increase in maximum speed (Aeronautics, 1913) and facilitated the flow of cool air relatively evenly over all four engines – motors and radiators (SA10, 1913). The engine motors would drive a tachometer – to measure the RPM (Revolutions per Minute) – via a malleable shaft from the motor to the pilot station dash. It was intended that the motors could be run or stopped during flight (SA10, 1913) as the power plant system had been designed for the aircraft to retain controllable flight with one of the engines shut down due to breakdown (Aeronautics, 1913). Exits from the fuselage to the wing were located on the fuselage sides to allow access to the engines in-flight for minor maintenance.

The S-21 Grand Baltic during early flight tests prior to modification to Russian Knight configuration. Note the passengers on the observation balcony forward of the enclosed cockpit. The new circle of heavier than air aviation quickly took note of the achievement of such a large aircraft being flown and the subsequent records, national (Imperial Russian) and international that were established by the design – including a world record for flight duration following the aircraft conversion to Russian Knight configuration.

Construction work on the Grand Baltic had commenced at the Baltic Carriage Works during 1912. The aircraft, which was built and prepared for flight through the first quarter of 2013 – various documentation would suggest the aircraft was completed on 4 March 1913 or 1 March 1913 (this date possibly refers to old style calendar). The maiden flight was conducted on 26 May 1913 (also stated as 27 April

1913). The aircraft had been prepared for flight at Hull Aerodrome, St. Petersburg, Russia. On the morning of the maiden flight, a crowd had begun to gather as news of the impending historic flight spread. The flight took place later that morning when the aircraft, at a weight exceeding 3 tons (3000 kg), climbed into the air (Rostec). On this historic occasion it was demonstrated that large size aviation would not, as some sceptics believed, remain the sole domain of aircraft employing lighter than air technologies – airships – which were being designed in increasingly larger, more powerful models in the same timeframe as that of the Grand Baltic (Russian Knight) and later the Ilya Muromets. During tests, a flight of 40 minutes duration was conducted over a distance of 90 km at an average altitude of 400 m whilst carrying five passengers. This flight was notable in that the air engineer climbed from the fuselage out onto the wing in order to demonstrate that the engines could be accessed while the aircraft was in flight.

Following modification the Grand Baltic, which was renamed Russian Knight, took on the unmistakable appearance of a four-engine biplane with the engines arranged on the wings, two either side of the central fuselage. In this configuration the aircraft continued flight testing in order to prove the concept of the large-multi engine aircraft.

The Grand Baltic/Russian Knight broke a number of Imperial Russian aviation records and an international record for passenger carrying ability. A notable flight took place on 1 August 1913, by which time the aircraft, following the modifications to the power plant configuration, was formally renamed Russian Knight (effective from June 1913). On this occasion the aircraft flew with seven passengers and established a word record for flight duration of around 2 hours (Sergeyev, History of Aviation Medicine, 1962), also stated as 1 hour 4 minutes (SA, 1913). Further notable flights included one carrying no less than twelve passengers on a flight duration of slightly in excess of 15 minutes (SA10, 1913 & l'Aerophile, 1913). These flights were obviously flown with higher load limits and passenger/crew numbers than originally planned. Flight testing had confirmed that the design was sturdy enough, with enough power, to provision for the movement of occupants around those areas of the aircraft accessible in flight without any corresponding detrimental effect on flight stability – this corresponded to movement of loads of up to 68 kg (~150 lb.) weight without affecting said flight stability (Aeronautics, 1913 & SA10, 1913).

There are several values forwarded for maximum speed attained by the Russian Knight. These range from 80 km/h up to 106 km/h (Zhemchuzhin *et al*, 1971, SA10, 1913, l'Aerophile, 1913 & Aeronautics, 1913). Somewhere in between is the most likely, perhaps in the late 80's to 90 km/h, following the engine modifications.

The major problem encountered during testing was the length of required take-off run. The available engine power enabled the aircraft to become airborne after a run of around ~183 m (600 ft.) or a little more, depending on ground surface (Aeronautics, 1913). Other values put take-off run at around ~213 m (700 ft.).

Emperor Nicholas II and Igor Sikorsky with Imperial Russian Army military pilots at Red Village, Russia, on 7 August 1913. MODRF

In a time before the proliferation of flat and firm airfields, there was no abundance of suitable surfaces available, restricting the fields available for operating such a large machine as the Grand Baltic/Russian Knight. It was determined that the vehicle was too heavy to operate from sand surfaces or soft ground as the wheels would sink into the ground due the aircraft excessive, for the time, weight. The problems associated with take-off were, in part, responsible for the change in the layout of the undercarriage units from one twin unit either side to two twin units either side – eight wheels in total (SA10, 1913). In comparison to typical aircraft of its time, no specific problems were encountered on landing the aircraft (Aeronautics, 1913) in either Grand Baltic or Russian Knight configurations.

There was military interest in the design from the earliest days, the 700 plus kg load able to be converted, in one manner or another, into an offensive bomb and defensive machine gun load, if this was desired, or for carriage of cameras for conducting photographic reconnaissance work. In the event, the Russian Knight was apparently purchased by the Imperial Russian Ministry of War (SA10, 1913), for its potential as a long-range aircraft for bombing, reconnaissance and general purpose operations, to be evaluated. This likely came about after Sikorsky's achievements with the Grand Baltic/Russian Knight had caught the attention of Tsar Nicholas II, whom was shown the aircraft at Tsarskoye Selo on 7 August 1913. The Tsar's interest in the aircraft may have been instrumental in the state Duma awarding a sum of 75,000 Tsarist Rubles in the form of a prize. It is unclear to what extent, if any, that this contributed to realising the grander project that was the Ilya Muromets.

The Russian Knight, although not progressing to serial production, was of considerable value in the development of large multi-engine aircraft. However, the aircraft operational life was limited due to an unfortunate mishap. On the occasion of a competition showcasing existing and potential military aircraft on 11 September 1913, an aircraft flown by Gaber-Volynsky was flying over the Russian Knight when, by chance, its engine broke loose and fell on the Russian Knight sat firmly on terra firma, destroying one of the wings. The aircraft was written-off following a decision not to repair it as Sikorsky concentrated on completing the S-22 Ilya Muromets. In excess of 50 flights had been logged on the Grand Baltic/Russian Knight, paving the way for future multi-engine developments at the Baltic Carriage Works in the shape of the S-22 to S-27 Ilya Muromets series of large multi-engine long range bomber/reconnaissance aircraft.

Sikorsky (right side) with Imperial Russian Army Cavalry General A.V. Kaulbars (centre) and an unidentified gentleman (left side) on Russian Knight balcony on the occasion of the third competition of military aircraft on 11 September 1913. Rostec

2

ILYA MUROMETS

The Grand Baltic/Russian Knight paved the way for the Ilya Muromets (Илья Муромец) – Ilya Muromets, also known as Ilya of Murom is a figure from Russian Folklore, a prominent Knight and defender of the court of tenth century Vladimir I of Kiev – the second four engine aircraft to be designed by Sikorsky and built at the Baltic Carriage Works. This design would go on to become the world's first serial produced four engine aircraft, spanning several variants. When the S-22 Ilya Muromets prototype was prepared for its maiden flight toward the end of 1913, it was the world's largest fixed wing aircraft then in existence (FYSAC, 1970).

Under the design leadership of Sikorsky, build of the prototype Ilya Muromets commenced in St. Petersburg in 1913. This was accomplished with the participation of others, notably N.N. Polikarpov (FYSAC, 1970) whom would go on to build military aircraft under the Polikarpov label in the early Soviet period. The S-22 Ilya Muromets, which was designed to have the potential for both military and civilian uses, primarily bomber and passenger carrying roles, was, like its Russian Knight predecessor, of wooden construction biplane layout with the engines installed on rigs on the lower wing. Studies were apparently conducted on a triplane layout, but preliminary data indicated no useful advantage of such a configuration, which would have had the disadvantage of increasing weight. The S-22, with an overall length of around ~19.81 m (~65 ft.), a wingspan of ~36.88 m (121 ft.) across (Rostec value states 31 m (101 ft.)) and chord, in the order of 9 ft., was notably larger than the Russian Knight. Available lifting area was almost ~185.8 m^2 (2000 $ft.^2$) (various values are in circulation, the most reliable being in the order of ~181.17 m^2 (1,950 $ft.^2$), dating from 1914 and apparently originating from the design team in that year. The tail section, located at the extreme rear of the fuselage, consisted of a number of control systems – a large surface area tail-plane elevator and three place rudder complex, total area being in the order of ~5.1 m^2 (55 $ft.^2$) (SA, 1914).

The S-22 undercarriage gear consisted of a skid complex with a smaller skid at the rear, below the tail section. Skids were incorporated into the design as the initial test phase was due to be conducted during the Russian winter, when available take-off/landing fields would be heavily snow/ice covered. Wheeled main undercarriage units would be incorporated into the design later. This consisted of a chassis accommodating a quartet of large wheels attached to an elastic shock-absorption complex. The introduction of wheels was instrumental in overcoming the unacceptably high friction that could be encountered by skids during take-off and landings (SA, 1914). A Dual skid/wheel undercarriage complex would be incorporated into series produced Ilya Muromets aircraft of the S-23 Series.

A common trait for all Ilya Muromets variants, S-22 through S-27, was the large enclosed cockpit cabin section, notwithstanding ports for defensive armament in the operational bomber role.

    As was the case with the Russian Knight, the fuselage of the Ilya Muromets was completely enclosed from the elements. The internal fuselage measured around 1.82 m (~6 ft.) in height and some 1.67 m (~5.5 ft.) in diameter at the bow section. The pilots(s) cabin was located in the nose section, ahead of the passenger/cargo compartment(s). Passenger accommodation was on a grander, more lavish scale than the already lavish, for the time, accommodation provided by the Russian Knight and any other aeroplane then flying or planned. Seating was provided for up to fifteen passengers and a small berth area was provided for a few sleeping passengers or crew, with a small compartment for a toilet facility located further aft. (SA, 1914). Wind generators provided electric supply for cabin lighting (Rostec) and power for cabin heating was generated by exhaust transferred from the four wing mounted (two either side of the fuselage) engines, each generating around 120-140 hp. (SA, 1914).

    The S-22 prototype was powered by four German developed and built Argus aero engines with a combined output of up to 560 hp. The Argus engine had been developed by the Imperial German firm, Argus Motoren Gesellschaft, which came into being in 1902. The first Argus engine was built in 1906, leading to engine developments that would power much of the first generation of German fixed wing aircraft and a number of foreign aircraft designs, particularly during the period 1910-1913 (Smithsonian). The availability of suitable German built Argus engines had been instrumental in realising the potential of the S-21 Grand Baltic (Russian Knight) and later the S-22 Ilya Muromets.

Ilya Muromets bomber aircraft modification with duel wheel/skid undercarriage complex. MODRF

The Argus, in various modifications, was a reciprocating (rotary) six cylinder in-line water cooled engine. Typical ratings were in the order of 120-150 hp. for the early variants that powered the Grand Baltic/Russian Knight and S-22 Ilya Muromets. The four Argus engines mounted on the Ilya Muromets could be started simultaneously or individually by a compressed air starting device controlled from the pilot's cabin. As was the case with the Russian Knight, it was possible to stop and restart individual engines whilst the aircraft was airborne. The power of the engines had to be sufficient to provide a maximum speed in the order of 112 km/h (~70 mph) in order to overcome headwinds in conditions below gale force. In operation, the Argus engines produced power in the order of around 1 hp. per 2.7 kg (~5 lb.) weight of engine and associated equipment/fuel (some 907 kg (~2,000 lb.) in regard to the Argus) (SA, 1914). This level of power provided the Ilya Muromets with the necessary performance to conduct the bomber, reconnaissance or transport roles with a respectable load carriage capability.

Interior of the cabin walkways of an undetermined Ilya Muromets variant.

While the sufficient power provided by the Argus engines made the aircraft more stable in high wind gusts than was the case for smaller aircraft, the controls were significantly harder for pilots to operate, requiring increased effort, due to the large area of the aircraft control systems. Stress loadings, which were a concerning factor in the design of large aeroplanes, was, at around 2.7 kg (~5 lb.) per square inch, significantly lower than many small size aircraft then flying (SA, 1914). The fear that loadings would be so high that unacceptable stresses would be exerted, were, therefore, alleviated in early tests.

The cockpit section of an Ilya Muromets with the pilots wheel (this page). Variant is not identified, but appears to be a **V/(B)** model.

The Ilya Muromets prototype conducted its maiden flight on 23 December 1913 (Russian Air Force (Aerospace Forces) Historical Archives for 23 December 1914). Two days later the aircraft established a load carrying record by lifting a payload of 1100 kg (1.1 tonne) into the air (TASS). On 12 February 1914, the aircraft was flown at altitudes up to 200 m with seventeen passengers – 16 human and a single Feline (domestic Cat), also stated to be a Dog – for a duration of 12 minutes. This established for the aircraft a world record in load carrying ability at that time. This was an encouraging beginning for the new chapter of heavy aviation in Russia. Other notable early flights included a 6 hour 33 minute duration flight in March 1914, during which the aircraft attained an altitude of 1650 m whilst carrying a load of 10 passengers (Sergeyev, History of Aviation Medicine, 1962). On 17 June 1914, the second Ilya Muromets aircraft demonstrated the range/payload potential of the design by conducting a flight from St Petersburg to Kiev (Imperial Russia - now an independent state of the former Soviet Union) – a distance of 1100 km was flown on the round trip, which included a refueling in Kiev (Rostec). This flight of the second aircraft, apparently fitted with Argus engines producing slightly more power than that available on the first Ilya Muromets, was instrumental in influencing the decision to adopt the design as a military aircraft – long-range bomber and reconnaissance.

Overall, with the Ilya Muromets, Sikorsky had succeeded in building an aircraft significantly larger and heavier than the Russian Knight, and one possessing higher performance in speed, altitude and load carrying capability – at around 1500 kg, load carrying capability was in the order of twice that of its predecessor.

Ground personnel run across the snow covered field as the Ilya Muromets prototype approaches for landing, or during an overflight of the field, with passengers standing on the outside of the aircraft structure.

Early variants of the Ilya Muromets could be equipped with wheeled and skid undercarriage complexes, whilst later variants were predominantly wheeled in regard to the main undercarriage system, retaining a skid system for the tail undercarriage unit.

The Svyatogor, designed by a team led by V.A. Slyersaryeb, was a truly gargantuan machine by the standards of the time.

Other Russian aircraft designers were working on creating heavy multi-engine aircraft, notably V.A. Slyersaryeb whom designed the Svyatogor, a large four engine machine which exceed the Ilya Muromets in overall dimensions and weight, and ultimately featured a higher load carrying capacity than Sikorsky's aircraft. The Svyatogor had a wing area of 190 m², a normal weight of 6500 kg and was to be powered by two engines, each with a power output of 450 hp.

Although flying some considerable time after the maiden flight of the Ilya Muromets, design of the Svyatagor had commenced in 1913, under a team headed by Slyersaryeb, whom had experience of large aircraft design/build, having been part of Sikorsky's team designing the Grand Baltic/Russian Knight (Zhemchuzhin *et al*, 1971). The Svyatogor was built in prototype form only, conducting its maiden flight in 1916 (Sergeyev, History of Aviation Medicine, 1962), by which time the Ilya Muromets had established itself in service as the world's premier large-size multi-engine, long range fixed wing bombing/reconnaissance aircraft.

Planning for the application of aviation to military uses in Imperial Russia had commenced in the 1880's, initially in the form of a Commission in the early part of that decade. This Commission was replaced by a number of non-military organisations, including the VII Aeronautical Department of the Imperial Russian Technical Society. It had been recognised by some individuals that Russia had allowed herself to fall behind other major European powers in the application of balloons to military roles. In this regard, in autumn 1884, Major General L.L. Lobko wrote to the Chief of the General Staff of the Russian Army, General (Infantry)

N.N. Obrtuchev, urging the formation of an aeronautics company along with a Commission that would look into the science of aeronautics from a military perspective – such a Commission came into effect on 5 January the following year and an aeronautics unit was formed on 7 February 1885 (VAGSh (Lashkov)).

Previous page: The Russian Falcon hot air balloon is raised into the air in 1885. This page: The first practical employment of airpower by Imperial Russia occurred when observations balloons were used during the Russo-Japanese war of 1904-1905. Here a balloon ascends for observation at Liaoyang City in August 1904. MODRF

As was the case with the other powers that would become embroiled in the Great War of 1914-1918, military aviation in Imperial Russia was in its infancy. Germany declared war on Russia on 1 August 1914 (the Austria-Hungarian Empire entered the war against Russia on 5 August 1914) in the opening phase of a conflict what would come to be known as the Great War (later referred to as World War 1). In the short period immediately preceding the outbreak of war, a training Corp was established at Gatchina to prepare for operations with ten Ilya Muromets aircraft that had been ordered for delivery to the Russian Army by the Baltic Carriage Works. At this time the aircraft were not planned to be concentrated into a squadron establishment, but rather distributed piecemeal among five or so Fortress Commands, each of which would receive two Ilya Muromets aircraft, along with a number of light aircraft (VAGSh (Lashkov), 2019). As war clouds were gathering across Europe, preparations for formation of a heavy bomber capability for the Russian Army was, in July 1914, further advanced through authorisation for the establishment of the Ilya

Muromets Airplane Command. This was to be set up with an establishment of one military official, four officers and 40 subordinate ranks. Planning called for each of the Ilya Muromets machines and their supporting light aviation and ground elements to be considered as equivalent to a Russian Army field squadron. This would mean that each Fortress Command would have the equivalent of two aviation tasked field squadrons. The respective field squadrons would be under the command of the headquarters of the respective field armies of the Fortress Commands. The formation of the first Ilya Muromets equipped units (apparently four) each equipped with at least one Ilya Muromets aircraft (referred to in Russian parlance as airships) and two or three light aircraft, was authorised by the Imperial Russian Minister of War (following approval of such by the Tsar, Nicholas II) in a resolution adopted by the Imperial Russian Military Council. Each of the Ilya Muromets units would be commanded by the command pilot of the Ilya Muromets aircraft (VAGSh (Lashkov), 2019).

Summer through winter 1914 and into 1915 was spent preparing for formation of a training syllabus and progression to operational units equipped with Ilya Muromets heavy bombers. MODRF

On 1 August 1914, the date Germany declared war on Russia, training of air and ground personnel for the planned Ilya Muromets bomber force was transferred, in command structure, from OVSh to what was termed the VAS (Military Aviation School). On the 19th of the month, an order, only the second emanating from the

Military Aviation School, authorised the establishment of the four previously referred to Ilya Muromets units, which would be commanded by Ilya Muromets commanders E.V. Rudnev (captain), S.M. Bradovich (captain), A.V. Pankratyev (Lieutenant) and S.L. Modrakh (Lieutenant). At this time a department was set up within the Military Aviation School, which would oversee the flight training on Ilya Muromets aircraft. The overall training syllabus was conducted under the command of Captain G.G. Gorshkov, whom was appointed the Deputy Commander of the Gatchina Aviation School (VAGSh (Lashkov), 2019).

The mechanism that would lead to formation of heavy bomber/reconnaissance squadrons, equipped with Ilya Muromets bomber/reconnaissance aircraft, was formally put in place on 23 December 1914 when Tsar Nicholas II authorised the decision that had been arrived at by the Military Council for the splitting of army aviation into light and heavy divisions. The light aviation would be under the command of individual army Corp whilst the heavy aviation (Ilya Muromets) would be under the direct command of the Headquarters of the Supreme Commander of the Army. Initial combat use called for the aircraft to operate in single-ship missions. Doctrine later evolved, resulting in a decision to form multi-aircraft units (de-facto bomber squadrons) with Mikhail Shidlovsky (an industrial figure taken directly from the civilian role as Chairman of the Board of the Baltic Carriage Works and handed the rank of Major-General) as overall commander. These decisions had been taken by the Military Council, subordinate to the Minister of War, on 21 December 1914 and approved by the Tsar on the 23rd of the month (noted above) (VAGSh (Lashkov), 2019 & Russian Air Force (Aerospace Forces) Historical Archives for 23 December 1914). When a long-range aviation capability had first been mooted to support the Russian army, it had initially been considered as a potential tool for solving reconnaissance tasks – equipped with a battery of cameras – rather than as a bomber force. The 23 December 1914 decision paved the way for the successive Ilya Muromets variants to be developed primarily as long range bomber aircraft with reconnaissance as a supporting/secondary role.

Toward the end of 1914, the newly formed Ilya Muromets air squadron was designated to be forward based near Staraya Jablonna, a village in the Kingdom of Poland. The first operational Ilya Muromets mission was flown in February 1915 (Russian Air Force (Aerospace Forces) Historical Archives for February 1915). This mission, flown in an aircraft commanded by Second-Captain Gorshkov, was conducted against German target(s) in East Prussia. Following several missions behind the German Frontal areas, the new threat that was the Russian heavy bomber force became clear to the German high command. To this end, a number of German counter raids were apparently flown against the Russian bomber base. Such raids were responsible for accelerating the organisation and deployment of dedicated Russian anti-aircraft units to defend against air attack. The German counter raids failed to curb the development of what was then an air squadron formation referred to as a Directorate, into an air squadron in being, as the Ilya Muromets establishment built up to a strength of twelve aircraft (VAGSh (Lashkov), 2019).

To support/protect the planned fleet of Russian aircraft conducting reconnaissance and bombing missions, and to mitigate against enemy reconnaissance and bombing aircraft, formation of Russia's fighter aircraft air arm was authorised by an order of the High Chief on 12 March 1916, paving the way for formation of three dedicated fighter units (MODRF, Russian Air Force (Aerospace Forces), Historical records). On 24 January 1915, around 14 months prior, the maiden flight of the prototype of the S-16 single-engine fighter aircraft (designed by Sikorsky) was conducted at the Baltic Carriage Works. The S-16 was designed as an escort fighter able to accompany Ilya Muromets bomber/reconnaissance aircraft operating individually or in formations (Russian Air Force (Aerospace Forces) Historical Archives for 24 January 1915). In the event, the large fleet of Ilya Muromets that was so desired did not materialise due to the realities on the ground – funding shortages, priorities for other aircraft types for other roles and hardships acquiring sufficient materials and engine stocks to power a large fleet of heavy bombers. Russia was heavily reliant on her Entente allies, Britain and France, for the supply of aircraft and engines. This was fraught with difficulties in the supply chain and changing priorities among supplier nations, sometimes leading to delays in acquisition or outright cancellation of deliveries. The problem was exacerbated after the October 1917 revolution when the supply of war materials to Russia was reconsidered and then reversed by her western allies. The unfortunate irony of the situation for Russia was that delays and cancellations of allied aircraft deliveries to Russia, such as the DH4 light bomber aircraft, increased pressure on indigenously procured aircraft like the Ilya Muromets, which were themselves reliant on allied supplied engines, as noted above.

The S-16, the prototype of which conducted its maiden flight on 24 January 1915, was developed at the Baltic Carriage Works as an escort fighter to accompany Ilya Muromets bombers. This fighter introduced synchronised machine gun firing through the propeller arc. MODRF

Production of a large fleet of Ilya Muromets bombers was fraught with problems that would prove difficult to overcome. During the war years up to the October 1917 Revolution, there were fifteen or so major aircraft production plants in Imperial Russia. These were spread between Moscow, Odessa, Petrograd (St. Petersburg was renamed Petrograd in 1914), Riga, Rybinsk, Simferopol and Taganrog. Most orders filled by Russian aircraft plants were for machines of foreign design, such as the French Farman, Moran and Nieuport. On a smaller scale was the production of machines of Russian design, including, Lebed, Parasol, S-16 and Ilya Muromets, the latter manufactured at the Russo-Baltic Railroad Car Plant (Baltic Carriage Works) in Petrograd, from where the design originated (MODRF, 2020 & FYSAC, 1970).

The Imperial Russian Army had on strength around 250 or so serviceable aircraft when war broke out in late July 1914. By the time of the October Revolution in 1917, the operational fleet consisted of around 1,000 aircraft, many of which were in dire need of repair. This unfavourable position was further exacerbated by the withholding by the Western allies of aircraft, engines and armaments ordered by Russia from those countries (FYSAC, 1970). The reality of the situation within the overall allied aircraft/engine production schedules and requirements was that of insufficient availability of high powered engines for large aircraft and rigid airships, even through 1917. This meant that a large production run for Ilya Muromets type aircraft was well-nigh impossible in Imperial Russia. While the western allies would later embark upon large-scale production of heavy bombers, as late as of 31 March 1917, Britain's Royal Naval Air Service had only 12 large multi-engine Handley Page 0/100 bombers in service (A.B. 163/9., 1917). The engine requirements for the twin engine Handley Page aircraft were half that per machine than it was for a four engine aircraft of the Ilya Muromets type. Other equipment for aircraft was in short supply in Russia. Due to demands for domestic consumption, the British Air Board refused a Russian request for 6,000 air guns (A.B.153/23., 1917), exacerbating the already difficult program for arming aircraft of various modifications. In October 1917, fifty DH4 light bombers, on order for the Russian government (agreed by the Colonel Yakowleff, the commander of the Russian Air Service) to augment their bombing capability, was postponed with Russian consent. In its stead, a new order was formulated for 75 DH4 to be delivered in spring 1918, allowing the 50 DH4, previously planned for delivery in winter 1917, to be allocated to the British RFC (Royal Flying Corp) (A.B.153/37., 1917). In the event, the DH4 order was not fulfilled. Following the October 1917 Revolution, the unstable political situation in Russia, and uncertainty over her future direction in prosecuting the war or making peace with Germany, led to the withholding of materials previously intended for transfer from her western allies. This involved engine orders, particularly 3,500 Hispano-Suiza engines ordered from the French government (A.B.153/35., 1917), but would affect the potential for future orders for other engine types.

There are no surviving documents that give a definitive number of Ilya Muromets built. However, it is known that at least sixty such machines were built, although some estimates put this at 70 plus. The Central Museum of the Russian Air Force states that 73 Ilya Muromets aircraft were built in total (CAFMM). This total may not be accurate, but it would certainly be in the general vicinity of total numbers built.

The S-25 (G-2 and later G-3), which first took to the air circa March 1916, introduced enhanced defensive capability through addition of a machine gun firing position in the aircraft tail section.

It appears that perhaps up to two additional S-22 aircraft were built after the first. However, contradictory statements/documentation make this problematic to qualify. What is clear is that at least two distinct S-22 aircraft conducted flight testing. The S-23 constituted a series produced variant(s) built during 1914-1915, also known as the B series. The S-23 also produced the V series, referred to as a modified B series (there is uncertainty in the designations systems as the Russian language V translated to the English language B, both variants potentially being one in the same). The G series, which followed the B/V Series, was the most numerous built, itself constituting a number of sub-variants – G-1 (S-24) and the G-2 and G-3 (S-25). The penultimate variant, carrying the designation S-26, covered the reduced power D Series with the S-27 designation being applied to what became known as the E Series. This final variant was the heaviest and carried the most powerful engines, each of which was rated at 220-270 hp. Basic dimensions of the various serial produced variants ranged from a length of just over 17 m for the G Series to just over 18 m for the E Series. Wingspans of the respective variants ranged, but were generally in the region of 30 m – the B/G and E Series were in excess of 30 m.

The succession of models reflected efforts to introduce improvements to the basic design, the E Series Ilya Muromets being credited with a maximum speed of 135 km/h and an operational ceiling of 4000 m. The maximum payload of 2500 kg included the crew of seven. Offensive load was in the region of 800 kg of bombs and defensive armament consisted of up to eight medium machine guns, positioned for defensive fire against attack by fighter aircraft (FYSAC, 1970).

Top: **An Ilya Muromets bomber is manhandled into position by ground personnel. Centre and bottom: Ilya Muromets bomber mock-up displayed at the Central Museum of the Russian Air Force, Monino.** MODRF/CAFMM

Whilst the speed values for the Argus powered Ilya Muromets prototype can be qualified, there are uncertainties as to the actual speeds attained by the series produced variants. However, it is possible to provide qualitative assessments based on estimated engine power output and rough take-off weights. It is the clear that the S-23 of the B series, with a similar take of weight to that of the S-22 and powered by four engines of around 135-150 hp., would have been endowed with a maximum flight speed of in the region of 100 km/h/± 5 km/h, depending on configuration and load carriage etc. The S-23 of the V Series would have operated at similar weights, possibly slightly higher, than the B Series, but would potentially have attained higher speeds – perhaps 10-15 km/h – more than the B Series due to increased engine power (this power may been a retrofit of B series). This would also have applied to the S-26, which operated at similar weights and with similar engine power to that of the V series. The S-25 (G Series) and S-27 (E Series) operated at weights of just above 6000 kg and 7460 kg respectively. These variants, powered by engines of 220-270 hp., could attain speeds in the region of 130 km/h.

Inset of previous page centre photograph shows positioning of engines on Ilya Muromets port wing. Later models of the Ilya Muromets were powered by models of the Sunbeam aero engine, which were arranged in a similar manner to that of the Argus engine powered Ilya Muromets. CAFMM

With the outbreak of World War 1, the supply of German Argus engines for future build Ilya Muromets beyond the initial development/production batch would no longer be possible, therefore, a suitable alternative power plant had to be sourced. As there was no suitable engine available from domestic Russian sources, the Argus replacement engine would have to be foreign sourced from one of Imperial Russia's entente allies, France or Great Britain. The Renault built Sunbeam engines appear to have been the major type powering the G and E Series. It would appear that thirty Sunbeam Crusader engines were ordered to power Ilya Muromets aircraft. This IS a small number considering four such units were required for each aircraft. It can be concluded that further engines were definitely acquired from French industry to power the bulk of Ilya Muromets aircraft built during 1916 and those reaching operational units in 1917, the Renault Sunbeam powering late series aircraft being rated at 270 hp.

The Sunbeam Crusader (designed by L. Coatalen) had its origins in an aero engine developed from the Sunbeam racing car engine that had won the European Grand Prix. The Aero engine emerged as an 8-cylinder 'V' configuration, referred to as a V-8, which was considered the optimum for reducing engine weight (around 425 lb., including the carburetor) through reduced length of the crankcase and crankshaft. Power output of the Sunbeam Crusader was in the order of 150 hp. when running at 2,500 RPM (Revolutions per Minute) – such an RPM was too high for the most efficient operation of the two-blade wooden propeller, therefore, a 2 to 1 gear system was incorporated into the crankcase, reducing rpm by around 50% (The Engineer, 1913). The engine could be considered a quantum leap in technology at that time for the facilitation of long duration/long-range flights, as it featured a low fuel consumption rate of just under half a pint of aviation fuel per brake horsepower per hour. This could equate to either increased flight duration/range or, alternatively, to reduced fuel load, which in turn decreased take-off weight requirements.

The Crusader entered flight test proper in October 1913. Following some bumps in the road, the engine design entered into a protracted flight test program in December that year. Sunbeam Crusader engines would go on to power a number of aircraft types, including the Royal Aircraft Factory RE.5 biplane and the Maurice Farman two seat biplane on a trials basis and the Short 827 seaplane and, of course, the Ilya Muromets.

Ilya Muromets – data furnished by CAFMM

Engine: Renault Sunbeam rated at 270 hp.
Crew: 4-8
Take-off weight: 3500 kg to 7460 kg
Maximum speed: 86-130 km/h
Ceiling: 500-4600 m
Machine gun armament: 3-8 (3-7 was more typical)
Standard bomb load: 190-480 kg (up to 800 kg could be carried)
Load carrying capacity: 1500 kg (included crew and stores)

Among the western Allies facing the Central Powers, Italy and Russia's Entente partner, Britain, commenced build of large multi-engine bombers several years after Russia. The Handley Page 0/400 had a weight of 6452 kg, similar to most Ilya Muromets variants, whilst the Italian Caproni CA.42 was heavier than the 0/400 and, at a speed of ~158 km/h (98 mph), was faster (Loftin, NASA SP-468, 1985). Both these designs, like the Ilya Muromets variants, were significantly heavier than the German Gotha, which had a typical weight in the region of 3600 kg. While these aircraft were inferior to the Ilya Muromets in some respects, they were superior in others, such as increased maximum speed. However, they were in effect a generational jump in that, in the case of the 0/400, they did not enter service until 1918, by which time the Ilya Muromets major period of combat employment had ended. The advantage of the 0/400, other than higher speed, was that it could haul a ~907 kg (2,000 lb.) bomb load to a target ~483 km (300 miles) distant. In excess of 400 0/400 bombers were delivered before the Armistice in November 1918 brought active hostilities in World War 1 to a close. Only 46 Handley Page 0/100 twin-engine bombers were delivered, the type not entering operational use until March 1917, more than two years after the first operational mission flown by the Ilya Muromets.

Handley Page 0/400 heavy bomber at East Fortune Royal Naval Air Service station on the Scottish East Coast in 1918. NMS

OPERATIONS – As summer 1915 wore on and the front line moved, the Ilya Muromets squadron transferred eastward to an airfield near the Russian city of Lida (now in modern day Belarus). It was from this base that an experimental mission was flown on 3 August 1915, with an S-23 V Series bomber carrying a large air bomb of 400 kg weight – becoming the first aircraft to carry such a weapon into the air (CAFMM). The successful employment of this large bomb led to development of an even larger weapon (640 kg) by the Baltic Shipyard in 1916. Such weapons were built with the intention of bombing the German submarine base located at Libava (Liepaja), Imperial Russia (now in modern day Latvia) (VAGSh (Lashkov), 2019).

Ilya Muromets aircraft of the Imperial Russian Army air service operated on several fronts facing the Central Powers during World War 1. Although their numbers in operational units was relatively small in comparison to other types, the presence of the Ilya Muromets heavy bomber fleet allowed bombing and reconnaissance missions to be conducted at considerable distances behind the lines of the opposing forces. MODRF

Top: Bomb production industry in Imperial Russia, despite being less prolific than that of her western allies, was able to produce standard air dropped bombs ranging from very small up to 400 kg class, as well as special operations weapons of 600 kg class. **Bottom:** An S-23 V Series Ilya Muromets heavy bomber carrying a 400 kg bomb suspended beneath the central fuselage.

In autumn 1915, the squadron moved to a base near Pskov on the Northern Front. As winter approached, a second Ilya Muromets squadron formed, this replacing the first squadron detachment on the Northern Front. The first squadron was now placed under the command (on a temporary basis) of the Russian Third

Army fighting on the South Western Front. A short time later the first detachment wound up combat operations due to the withdrawal of equipment. On 4 December 1915, Order No.272, issued by the Supreme Commander in Chief, authorised the established strength of the Ilya Muromets air squadron to be increased to twenty aircraft, allowing for the establishment of three separate combat detachments. Within the structure of the squadron was an establishment of up to fourteen light aircraft and an integral anti-aircraft defence detachment for base defence. By the time the 1915 air campaign closed, the Ilya Muromets squadron had flown around 100 combat missions, during the course of which in excess of 19500 kg of bombs had been dropped on enemy targets. With the success of the Ilya Muromets on operations, the decision was taken to increase the combat strength to around thirty operational bombers during the course of 1916 (VAGSh (Lashkov), 2019).

Operations continued on the South-Western Front. Among the notable contributions of the Ilya Muromets force to the war effort was a number of missions flown against Astro-Hungarian positions, commencing a day or so before the start of the 1916 Brusilov offensive (4 June to 10 August 1916). Among the targets attacked were transportation hubs, including railway junctions, to disrupt the ability of the Austria-Hungarian forces to reinforce their front positions. As the 1916 campaigns wore on into the autumn, the Ilya Muromets squadron operating on the South Western Front moved to a headquarters base area in the vicinity of the Imperial Russian city of Vinnitsa (now in modern day Ukraine). At some point following the Romanian (Rumanian) entry into the war on the side of the Entente powers, Russia deployed a detachment of Ilya Muromets bombers in that country to provide support to the Danube Army (VAGSh (Lashkov), 2019).

Many missions called for carriage of large loads of small anti-personnel bombs, here being loaded onto an Ilya Muromets bomber sporting the Imperial Russia side flash.

In the new operational theatre, the Ilya Muromets force flew 156 operational sorties, during the course of which almost 19000 kg of bombs were dropped on enemy targets. Documentation shows that up to 39 Ilya Muromets aircraft were in the inventory during 1916 campaigns, but it is unclear if this is the number of new machines delivered that year or if this was the total number on strength. The increased availability of Ilya Muromets machines led to an increase in the number of operational detachments to five and the number of available crews increased to 35 operational and five for Ilya Muromets aircraft allocated to the training syllabus. This was provisionally authorised in a regulation emanating from the Chief of the Staff of the Supreme-Commander-in Chief of the Imperial Russian Army in February 1917 (VAGSh (Lashkov), 2019).

The E Series (S-27) was overall the heaviest of the Ilya Muromets variants to enter serial production. Rostec

February 1917 was the month that a Revolution shook Russia and caused concern within her Entente allies. There were consequences as to how the heavy aviation elements – Ilya Muromets Squadron(s) – would function. The squadron now came under the command of the Field Directorate of Aviation and Aeronautics within the Headquarters of the Supreme Commander-in-Chief of the Russian Army. The war effort of the Ilya Muromets squadron was conducted on the South Western and Romanian Fronts during 1917. In the build up to the Russian offensive of June 1917, the Heavy Aviation (Ilya Muromets detachments) were employed on reconnaissance flights over the enemy rear areas. Once the offensive opened, the bombers commenced offensive bombing missions against key targets, including transport/communication links between the front lines and the rear supply areas. By the time the 1917 campaign closed the Ilya Muromets force had flown seventy or so operational sorties (it is unclear if this is the total number flown or if this refers only to bombing operations) during the course of which around 10400 kg of bombs were dropped on enemy targets (VAGSh (Lashkov), 2019).

Depending upon variant and role the Ilya Muromets operated with a crew of 4-8 and carried up to eight defensive machine guns and a typical offensive bomb load of 400 kg (Russian Air Force (Aerospace Forces) Historical Archives for 23 December 1914). One modification increased defensive armament to eight rifle calibre machine guns and a single cannon (undetermined calibre) (Zhemchuzhin *et al*, 1971), but this was by no means standard.

Ilya Muromets aircraft, despite their large size, which could be considered to translate into relatively easy targets, proved to be resilient to sustained attacks by ground fire or enemy fighter aircraft on operations. Air combat at the time involved getting very close to an enemy, often resulting in enemy fighter aircraft being thrown about through slipstream effects produced by the large bombers and the after-wash of the four engines. Only two Ilya Muromets aircraft are confirmed as having been brought down in the course of an air combat engagement, although a number of others suffered such severe damage that they were written off after returning to base or made emergency landings before reaching base.

What appears to be a G-2 or G-3 Series Ilya Muromets bomber operating in environmental conditions of heavy snow cover in 1917. This variant of the bomber featured the tail defensive gun position.

The Revolution of October 1917 (November in the Gregorian calendar), in which the Bolsheviks seized power from the provisional government that had been in place since the Revolution of February 1917, resulted in radical changes within Russian civil society and military organisations. This effected the Heavy Aviation (Ilya Muromets) fleet significantly. The Imperial Russian Province of Ukraine was granted broad sweeping autonomy by the new power base, leading to a large degree of what was referred to as 'Ukrainisation' of the Russian South Western and the Romanian Fronts. This resulted in those elements of the Heavy Aviation (Ilya Muromets Squadron) that were based at Vinnitsa (Ukraine) being placed under the command structure of the newly established Ukrainian political establishment (VAGSh (Lashkov), 2019). This depletion of the Heavy Aviation ranks through allocation of a number Ilya Muromets aircraft to Ukraine, along with the general disorganisation prevalent within the Russian Army following the October Revolution, resulted in the Ilya Muromets force falling into a state of disarray. To address the dire situation of Heavy Aviation those Ilya Muromets machines remaining with the Detachments of the Northern Groupings, still under Russian control, were reorganised as an element of the newly established Workers and Peasants Red Air Force early in 1918. The Ilya Muromets Heavy Aviation Air Squadron (at some point early in 1918 this label was reattached to the squadron) was initially based at Nizhny Novgorod, Russia, several hundred kilometers to the East of Moscow, Russia, before transferring to a base near the Russian city of Lipetsk, several hundred kilometers southward from Moscow. Changes in the command structure were introduced in autumn 1918 – operations of the squadron were conducted under the command of the Chief and Commissioner of the Air Force of the Southern Front, with higher command under the Field Directorate of Aviation and Aeronautics of the Army. Further unit designation changes were introduced, the squadron eventually becoming the Ilya Muromets Aircraft Division (VAGSh (Lashkov), 2019). During this upheaval, hostilities between Russia and the Central Powers officially ended on 15 December 1917, under the terms of the Brest-Litovsk Treaty. The Bolshevik government in Russia had previously ordered an end to military operations against the Central Powers and Turkey on 26 November that year (Britannica).

The chaos that followed the October 1917 revolution would propel Russia into a civil war. Air power in civil war Russia was a shadow of what it had been a few years prior. There was a shortage of production/servicing/repair centres, reducing the availability of aircraft to Bolshevik (Red Russian) forces fighting White Russian forces supported militarily by western nation, including Russia's former Entente allies, Britain and France. The importance of air power for the Bolshevik forces, although seriously hindered through lack of modern machines and manufacturing and servicing capacity, was fostered from the top down. As early as 1914/1915 (pre revolution), Vladimir Ilyich Lenin was an ardent proponent of the future of aviation as an integral element of the army in order to increase mobility and provide the ability to strike targets well beyond the reach of ground based artillery (The Break-up of the Il International, 1915 & Zhemchuzhin *et al*, 1971). The first use of airpower by the Bolsheviks (authorised by Lenin) was a leaflet drop by aircraft over the city of Petrograd (later renamed Leningrad and again, in the 1990's, renamed St Petersburg, the name it bore until 1914) on the second day of the October 1917 revolution. The first recorded bombing mission of the October 1917 Revolution period took place on the 28th of that month when aircraft attacked troops opposing the Revolution under the command of General Krasnov (Zhemchuzhin *et al*, 1971). These early beginnings of Red air power were further cemented with the establishment of a headquarters organisation, for controlling air operations, in Smolny, near Petrograd, in November 1917 and the All Russian Board of Republican Air Force Control was brought into being in December that year, with the specific function of forming aviation detachments of air equipment and personnel.

Previous page: An unidentified Ilya Muromets operating with Bolshevik forces during the Russian Civil War and the war against foreign interventionists. This page: Red Air Force Ilya Muromets Fighting Ship 5th – No.280 – (a G-2 or G-3 Series) in Sarapul, July 1920, just prior to being dispatched to a frontal area for operations against White Russian forces during the Russian Civil War. MODRF

A Heavy bombing/reconnaissance capability was made available by concentrating a handful of Ilya Muromets machines into what was termed a Special Purpose Aviation Group, the formation of which had been authorised by the Chairman of the Peoples Commissars of the RSFSR (Russian Soviet Federal Socialist Republic) Vladimir I. Lenin. This unit was tasked with conducting attacks against the Fourth Cavalry Corp, White Russian Army on the Don. This Corp had been conducting attacks on the rear areas of the Russian Red Army Southern Front. The first Civil War Combat mission involving an Ilya Muromets aircraft took place on 8 August 1919. In May the following year, the small force of Ilya Muromets, now referred to as the 1st detachment, commenced missions in support of the 16th Soviet Army operations against Polish troop positions and transportation/lines of communications on the Soviet-Polish Front. The Ilya Muromets would later be placed under the command of the Chief of Aviation of the 13th Soviet Army on the Southern Front (VAGSh (Lashkov), 2019).

The Ilya Muromets force flew sixteen sorties during the Russian Civil War. The small number of aircraft involved dropped a mere 2600 kg of bombs on enemy targets, as well as 192 kg of metal anti-personnel arrows and 105 kg of leaflets. Of the total sortie number, nine were flown on the Southern Front in the late Civil War period (VAGSh (Lashkov), 2019).

A sentry stands guard over an Ilya Muromets heavy bomber adorned with the red star that would become characteristic of Soviet and later Russian Federation military aircraft markings into the twenty first century.

The early Soviet period saw the aircraft of the Ilya Muromets Division involved more heavily in establishing air transport routes than it had been in bombing missions. Ilya Muromets aircraft were instrumental in establishing embryonic long-range air transport links within territories controlled by the Soviet Bolsheviks. An air route service linking Moscow, Oryol and Kharkov was established with Ilya Muromets aircraft on 1 May 1921 (Russian Air Force (Aerospace Forces) Historical

Archives for 1 May 1921 & Zhemchuzhin *et al*, 1971). This had been set up by a decree issued by the Council of Labour and Defence of the RSFSR. During the period covered by the temporary service, 1 May 1921 into early October 1921, a total of 43 transport air flights were conducted with the Ilya Muromets fleet, which carried some 2000 kg of cargo and 60 passengers. On the 17th of January that year, the foundations of air law governing the use of transport aviation, including that of foreign nations flying over Soviet territory, had been laid. This was followed by a bilateral treaty with Germany, referred to as Dyeruluft. This effectively established the Soviet-German Society of Air Communications, governing the establishment of aviation routes between both territories. This, in turn, led to the inauguration of an air link between Moscow and Konigsberg in German Prussia (modern day Russian enclave of Kaliningrad) – this route covered a distance in the region of 1300 km (Zhemchuzhin *et al*, 1971).

Top: Following retirement of the Ilya Muromets fleet, the Soviet air forces were deficient a large size long-range bomber capability until the advent of the Tupolev **TB-1 (ANT-4)**, which flew in 1925 and entered service in 1929. The TB-1 would pave the way for the **TB-3 heavy bomber**, which served into World War 2 in several roles, **including bomber and transport.** Tupolev

Whilst the air transport experiment was underway the Ilya Muromets Air Division remained a constituent part of the bomber/reconnaissance force. This remained the case until August 1922, when the poor state of the fleet led to the disbandment of the Division, although some aircraft and equipment was transferred to the School of Air Shooting and Bombing (Sepukhov) (VAGSh (Lashkov B), 2019) to prepare aircrews for future bomber units. Authorisation for development of a new twin engine heavy aircraft capable of conducting a bomber role was allocated to TsAGI (Central Aerodynamic Institute) by the Special Technical Bureau for Military Inventions in November 1924. A prototype for a twin-engine low-wing monoplane, designated ANT-4 (TB-1/R-3), conducted its maiden flight on 25 November the following year (pilot, A.I. Tomashevsky). Serial production commenced in summer 1929 and, with deliveries to operational bomber units, the embryonic Soviet Air Forces were able to commence the reconstitution and surpassing (aircraft of the ANT-4 type, although having a reduced load carrying capability compared with the Ilya Muromets series, were superior in most other respects) of the heavy bomber capability that had been proven with the Ilya Muromets fleet during World War 1 and the Russian Civil War. Other than flights with early development aircraft, the ANT-4 would be powered by a domestic designed and built power plant, thus eliminating the problem that had hampered Imperial Russia's ability to build up a large heavy bomber force during the war years of 1914-1917.

While a full-scale mock-up of an Ilya Muromets aircraft is displayed at the Central Museum of the Russian Air Force, Monino, Moscow, there are no surviving Ilya Muromets airframes left in existence. The Mock-up was received by the museum in 1979 and, following a period of restoration, was put on display in 1985 (CAFMM).

Although largely overlooked in historiography, in a real sense the Grand Baltic/Russian Knight and Ilya Muromets were the foundation stones for the large multi-engine transport and bomber/reconnaissance aircraft that proliferated in a diversity of roles, ranging from long-range strategic strike to long-range passenger transport, through the twentieth century and into the twenty first century. In 1999, an order emanating from the Commander in Chief of the Russian Federation Air Force moved that 23 December (in recognition of the date in 1914 of the authorisation for formation of the Ilya Muromets bomber squadron within the command of the Imperial Russian Army) would be the anniversary date of Long Range Aviation and declared as a national holiday in Russia. In 2021, the name of the pioneer of Long Range Aviation in 1914 Imperial Russia, Ilya Muromets, remains prominent in twenty first century Russia's Long Range Aviation, adorning the fuselage of a Tupolev Tu-160 White Swan (NATO reporting name 'Blackjack') variable-geometry strategic missile carrier – an element of the Russian Federations triad of nuclear deterrent forces. The Tu-160 was, in 2021, the largest mass combat aircraft in the world, just as the Ilya Muromets had been when it debuted in 1914.

Page 41-42: The Ilya Muromets heavy bomber is commemorated as a pioneer of Russian Long Range Aviation in the twenty first century. The name adorns the fuselage of a Tupolev Tu-160 White Swan variable-geometry strategic missile carrier of the Long Range Aviation of the Russian Federation Strategic Missile Forces in 2021. MODRF/UAC

GLOSSARY

CAFMM	Central Air Force Museum Monino
ft.	Feet (unit of measurement)
ft.^{2}	Feet squared
hp.	Horse power
kg	Kilogram
km	Kilometre
km/h	Kilometre(s) per hour
lb.	Pound (unit of weight)
m	Metre
m^2	Metres squared
MODRF	Ministry of Defence of the Russian Federation
mph	Miles per Hour
NASA	National Aeronautics and Space Administration
NMS	National Museums Scotland
RPM	Revolutions per Minute
RSFSR	Russian Soviet Federal Socialist Republic
TsAGI	Central Aerodynamic Institute
UAC	United Aircraft Corporation
VAGSh	Scientific Research Institute of Military History
$\pm$	Plus or minus
$\sim$	Approximately equal to (can also be used to mean asymptotically equal)

BIBLIOGRAPHY

A.B.153/23. Air Board Report to the Cabinet, 1917
A.B.153/35. Air Board Report to the Cabinet, 1917
A.B.153/37. Air Board Report to the Cabinet, 1917
A.B.163/9. *Developments in Organisation*, Air Board Report to the Cabinet, 31 March 1917
Aeronautics (1913) 'The Sikorsky Air Limousine', *Aeronautics, pp 106*, September 1913
Ilya Muromets Exhibit data sheet, Central Museum of the Russian Air Force
l'Aerophile (1913) 'Un Remarkable Aeroplane Russe: Le "Grande" de Sikorsky', l' Aerophile, pp 391-392, 1 September 1913
l'Aerophile (1914) 'Les Aerobus: Un nouvel apparel geant de Sykorsky', l' Aerophile, pp 137-138, 15 March 1914
Lashkov, A (2019) *Russian Air Power – Beginnings of Long Range Aviation*, VAGSh, Institute of Military History, Russian Federation Armed Forces
Lashkov, A (undated) *The first use of Aeronautical vehicles in combat*, VAGSh, Institute of Military History, Russian Federation Armed Forces
Lashkov, A (undated) *The Origins of the Russian Air Force*, VAGSh, Institute of Military History, Russian Federation Armed Forces
Loftin, L.K. (1985) 'The Quest for Performance: the evolution of modern aircraft', NASA SP-468, NASA Scientific and Technical Information Branch, Washington D.C.
MODRF Historical Archive for 23 December 1913
MODRF Historical Archive for 23 December 1914
MODRF Historical archive for 24 January 1915
MODRF Historical Archive for 18 June 1915
MODRF Historical Archive for 1 May 1921
MODRF (2012) *Creation of Military Air Forces of Russia and its development*, Research Institute (Military History) of the Military Academy of the General Staff of the Russian Armed Forces
Rostec (2020) *Russian Knight, by Engineer Sikorsky*, Rostec Corporation, Russian Federation
Russian Air Force (Aerospace Forces) Historical Archives for 3 February 1887
Russian Air Force (Aerospace Forces) Historical Archives for 22 February 1907
Russian Air Force (Aerospace Forces) Historical Archives for 30 July 1909
Russian Air Force (Aerospace Forces) Historical Archives for 19 June 1910
Russian Air Force (Aerospace Forces) Historical Archives for 24 February 1912
Russian Air Force (Aerospace Forces) Historical Archives for 12 March 1916
Scientific American (1913) 'The Biggest Flying Machine in the World: The Remarkable Biplane of Sikorsky', pp 280, Scientific American, 11 October 1913
Scientific American (1914) 'Sikorsky's Stupendous Biplane', pp 91, Scientific American Supplement No.1988, 7 February 1914
Sergeyev, A.A. (1962) 'Essays on the History of Aviation Medicine', USSR Academy of Sciences Publishing House, Moscow

Sikorsky Archives

TASS (2013) *Russia remembers 4-engine Ilya Muromets wooden biplane of a century ago*, TASS News Agency, Russia

The Engineer, 1913

Yakovlev, A.S. (1968) 'Fifty Years of Soviet Aircraft Construction', Translated from Russian, NASA TT F-627 c.1. Published for NASA & the National Science Foundation, Washington, D.C. by the Israel Program for Scientific Translations

Zhemchuzhin, N.A., Levin, M.A., Merkulov, I.A., Naumov, V.I., Pozhidayev, O.A., Frolov, S.P. & Frolov, V.S. (1971) 'Soviet Aircraft & Rockets', Original Russian Language publication in Moscow, translated version published For the National Aeronautics and Space Administration, and the National Science Foundation, Washington, D.C., Amerind Publishing, New Delhi, India

ABOUT THE AUTHOR

Hugh Harkins FRAS, MIstP, MRAeS is a physicist/historian and author with an extensive research/study background in aeronautic, astronautic, astrophysics, geophysics, nautical and the wider scientific, technical and historical fields. He is also involved in research in the field of Scottish history, which formed a significant element of dual undergraduate degrees. Hugh has published in excess of seventy books, non-fiction and fiction, writing under his given name as well as utilising several pseudonyms. He has also written for several international magazines, whilst his work has been used as reference for many other projects, ranging from the aviation industry, international news corporations and film media to encyclopaedias, museum exhibits and the computer gaming industry. Hugh is an elected Fellow of the Royal Astronomical Society and is an elected member of the Institute of Physics and Royal Aeronautical Society. He currently resides in his native Scotland. Other titles by the author include:

Russian/Soviet Aircraft Carrier & Carrier Aviation Design & Evolution Volume 1 - Seaplane Carriers, Project 71/72, Graf Zeppelin, Project 1123 ASW Cruiser & Project 1143-1143.4 Heavy Aircraft Carrying Cruiser

Soviet Mixed Power Experimental Fighter Aircraft – Piston-Liquid Propellant Rocket Engine/Piston-Ramjet/Piston-Pulsejet & Piston-Compressor Jet Engine Designs of the 1940's

Raid on the Forth - The First German Air Raid on Great Britain in World War II

Light Battle Cruisers and the Second Battle of Heligoland Bight

Russia's Coastal Missile Shield - Bal-E & Bastion Mobile Coastal Cruise Missile Complexes

Iskander - Mobile Tactical Aero-Ballistic/Cruise Missile Complex

Orbital/Fractional Orbit Bombardment System - The Soviet Globalnaya Raketa

Counter-Space Defence Co-Orbital Satellite Fighter

Russia's Strategic Missile Carrier/Bomber Roadmap 2018-2040 – PAK DA, Tu-160M2, Tu-95MSM & Tu-22M3M

Sukhoi T-50/PAK FA - Russia's 5th Generation 'Stealth' Fighter

Sukhoi Su-35S 'Flanker' E - Russia's 4++ Generation Super-Manoeuvrability Fighter

Sukhoi Su-30MKK/MK2/M2 - Russo Kitashiy Striker from Amur

MiG-35/D 'Fulcrum' F – Towards the Fifth Generation

Air War over Syria, Tu-160, Tu-95MS & Tu-22M3 - Cruise Missile and Bombing Strikes on Syria, November 2015-February 2016

Sukhoi Su-27SM(3)/SKM

X-35 – Progenitor to the F-35 Lightning II

X-32 - The Boeing Joint Strike Fighter

Boeing X-36 Tailless Agility Flight Research Aircraft

XF-103 – Mach 3 Stratospheric Interceptor Concept

North American F-108 Rapier - Mach 3 Interceptor

Convair YB-60 - Fort Worth Overcast

Into The Cauldron - The Lancaster MK.I Daylight Raid on Augsburg

Hurricane IIB Combat Log - 151 Wing RAF, North Russia 1941

RAF Meteor Jet Fighters in World War II, an Operational Log

Typhoon IA/B Combat Log - Operation Jubilee, August 1942

Defiant MK.I Combat Log - Fighter Command, May-September 1940

Blenheim MK.IF Combat Log - Fighter Command Day Fighter Sweeps/Night Interceptions, September 1939 - June 1940

Fortress MK.I Combat Log - Bomber Command High Altitude Bombing Operations, July-September1941

www.ingramcontent.com/pod-product-compliance
Lightning Source LLC
Chambersburg PA
CBHW050456110426
42743CB00017B/3390